L.I.F.E
on stages

a

poetry

performance

on

my

next

steps

after

adoption

Anthony Edge

Grosvenor House
Publishing Limited

This book is published by
Grosvenor House Publishing Ltd
Link House
140 The Broadway, Tolworth, Surrey, KT6 7HT.
www.grosvenorhousepublishing.co.uk

A CIP record for this book
is available from the British Library

Paperback ISBN 978-1-80381-681-4
Hardback ISBN 978-1-80381-682-1

Caution – This collection contains explicit language

For Mum and Dad, who gave me life.
For Josie, who gave me life again.

And for the window… of life.

'There's no such word as can't.'
—Doreen Edge

C.O.N.T.E.N.T.S

Introduction

Words mean so much, from those spoken to the ones written down. What you hold right now are words; about 7,000.

It was 1988, at the age of nine, when I used my words to ask the most important question I have ever asked (apart from 'Will you marry me?'): 'Am I really adopted?'

Fast forward over thirty years and I am sitting in a room reading through my adoption records, trying to understand the words on the page as well as those in my head.

The words in this collection are all about life's questions; What does it mean to be adopted? How did I get to middle age? And can you really have sex with a fridge? It features my highlights and my lowlights, bookended by the spoken word to the written on my adoption. It is the first of two books; a sneak peek behind the curtain of the memoir's performance, you might say. However, you don't have to wait for the second book, as life's too short; just like this book. It won't take you long to read it. Maybe you could read this sitting on a train (when there is no signal on your mobile), in ~~Starbucks~~ an independent coffee shop (still with no phone signal), or on the loo (with your mobile on charge in another room).

When you get to the end, ask yourself… how did the words make you feel? Were you left with answers, or questions? If it was answers, then I guess my work here is done. If you were left with questions, that means you want to know more, and hopefully buy my next book! I wanted to know more, because, although I had some answers, and the love of wonderful parents, I still had the biggest question unanswered; 'Who am I?'

At the age of forty-three, I went to find out.

Words mean so much... and these are mine.

An identity,
unwanted in the chamber -
the unspeakable.

Stage One

L.I.F.E

LOST IN MY SOUND
LOST IN MY VOICE
LOST IN WHO I WAS
LOST IN WHAT I HAD FOUND

IDENTITY IN THE PILLARS
IDENTITY IN THE PEWS
IDENTITY IN A BLACK ROBE
IDENTITY I THOUGHT I KNEW

FINDING MY WAY BACK
FINDING MY WAY HOME
FINDING OUT WHAT WAS OLD
FINDING OUT WHAT WAS NEW

ECHOES IN LETTERS
ECHOES IN A TIN
ECHOES OF MYSTERY
ECHOES OF HISTORY

After...

Still born, body of the unplanned,
that is where I began.
Conceived without meaning,
drifting from the womb like a lonely pebble,
living now as the shell of a man.

A reject, left in neglect.
Too broken to cement walls
in the foundation of lies
of a 'family'. Fostered in a 'family',
before they built life on the other side.

I saw a different name,
I saw the word 'abuse'
written down, a life I did not choose.
Pieces of my life recorded,
sitting in the place where I was adopted.

A place free from scarring,
banging my head to free the suffering.
With my family where I really began,
re-born in a home with feeling,
truth lived there, in walls of healing.

Ernie

Her name was Sue,
she lived at twenty-two.
I lived at twenty-one,
but could not poo.

Straining on the potty,
silence on the ground,
strained in my parents' eyes,
until we heard the sound.

The Fastest Milkman in the West!
The hoof beats pound,
pasteurised high as Sue's chest
from Ernie on his delivery round.

A song they couldn't stand,
but soon I would excrete,
Ernie hit the sky from stale pork pie,
my own delivery now complete.

There were tears all round,
Mum and Dad could get to bed,
Sue married a man named Ted,
poor Ernie was left for dead.

Thanks to a milkman, I was relieved!
Driving his cart around the west,
Ernie's words really moved me,
all the way through the northwest.

Stage Two

Lancashire

Dust 'ere?
Got thee a story
abeawt wen I wurr a lad.
As tutha kids ran t'sweetest place,
I ad owd o'mothers and,
walkin thru deserted land,
wurr foyer station use fot stand.
We'd open doower t'market,
nowt but noise had started.
Went for see mon, tha'knows,
who'd gimme a slice
of someweer I'd never been befoower
an owd it in palm o'thand.
These places sounded reet posh,
not from round 'ere.
From far and wide,
all stood side bi'side,
th'inside glass.
Cheshire 'n' Gloucester,
Wensleydale 'n' Leicester.
I took one closer,
one wi' crumbly texture,
th'omeland rapped in papper,
mi little taste o' Lancashire.

Grommets

Voiced for the silence,
drowned under waves
in those primary days.
Stretchered to the river
of intravenous dreams,
where numbers flowed
down tubes in the canal,
risen in streams of vomit,
risen in sounds from a grommet.

The Longest Night

'Twas the longest night on Christmas Eve,
for the little boy who did believe.
Others snoozed away with a sound of a snore,
happily wrapped up behind the bedroom door.
Mother and Father in one, Grandparents in another,
not a move till seven, staying under cover.
It was just the boy whose eyes stayed open,
thinking the morning would never happen.
Every hour the clock was aglow,
middle of the night was all it would show.
The little boy rose at the strike of three,
leaving the room, to see what he could see.
Taking a step, avoiding a creak,
creeping downstairs to take a peek.
He stared through pine to pine,
eyes catching a glimpse of sparkle and shine.
Then back to bed till the clock glowed seven,
time to wake up and open presents.
Grandad was gasping for tea,
Grandma was looking for teeth.
Mother and Father off for a wee,
before the little boy sat with his family.
Each present lay across the sheepskin,
leaving mystery to what was wrapped within.
Awakened with joy as others were still yawning,
to a Happy Christmas for all and all a good morning.

Carry On

Carry On,
said the Nurse, the Matron.
The Doctor told me to Carry On,
then he told me Again.

I heard it from the Girls; Cleo, Emmanuelle,
the boys; Henry, Jack and Dick said it as well.

The Sergeant made me march on,
but I was lost,
so the Constable gave me direction.

I couldn't understand
so the Teacher gave me education.

I carried on,
until the Cabby came,
Regardless of Convenience,
to drive me to my destination.

I went Abroad,
I went Cruising,
I went Camping
Up the Khyber, Up the Jungle,
dressed as a Cowboy,
to Follow that Camel.

Loving every moment
away from Spying faces,
Screaming voices in my mind.

I remembered when you Carry On,
you Don't Lose Your Head,
you think of England,
you never look Behind.

Stage Three

Body Parts

Scouring with the shovel,
in the boxes of bodies,
in the darkness of delights,
to taste that sweet skin and bone,
all reduced to fizz and foam.

Sheltering on gums, teeth,
underneath sweet lips.
Creatures got crushed,
trapped by spiders, snakes,
shrimps, mice huddled in the shakes.

Tearing at the tissues,
pulling at the heart,
at the ring of friendship.
With sugariness of cattle skin,
wool was worth sweetness of sin.

Devouring organs, intestines,
carefree of guillotined gelatine,
these were the juiciest body parts,
ripped apart for my pleasured fix,
animals were my pick 'n' mix.

ATLANTIC

Frequently shifting in the AM trying to find a
happy medium, until I finally tuned into your sound.

It was the long wave that brought me to
your noise, stationed to the crackle in your voice.
Echoing that the best things in life were free.
Forever associated, forever connected with my high school days,
with words joined together for the phrase that pays.

You brought joy, a smile, a sign, a wonder,
sleeping on streets, under satellites, under stars at midnight.

You were destiny, you were heaven, you were harmony,
with your rhythm, your red eyes, you were a
stranger, living in danger to where you would linger.
A lover, a dreamlover, an informer, with no limit.
You gotta be beautiful, too blind to see it,

No doubt ancient but better than the real thing.
You brought the weather with you, as the sun

was going down. We danced in those gold fields,
away from hazards of broken glass and achy hearts.
It was the perfect place to believe in dreams,
it was the perfect year to lay those tears,
at the end of the road were diamonds, pearls.

I wish I'd said please don't go, please stay,
because I missed you, I am missing you now.

I'd like to say I am doing fine now,
I wouldn't lie to you, all I wanna do
is remember the time, time to make you mine,
to be with you, just another day with you.
There was no one else I'd rather listen to.

The Squared Circle

Ladies and Gentlemen,
the following is about contests
that were scheduled for one fall,
for challenges,
for championships,
for superstars
who came down the aisle,
larger than life,
in spandex, in baby oil,
shaking ropes, flexing muscles,
stamping feet
to enhance their punches.

They came loud and wild,
to entertain
every man, woman and child.
A Hulk in yellow pants,
A Warrior in tassels,
A Hitman in sunglasses,
A Model spraying 'arrogance'.
There was a Macho Man, a Tax Man,
A Million Dollar Man.
A Snake, Bulldog, an Alligator,
A Matador, Mountie
and an Elvis impersonator.

They came from the future,
from parts unknown,
from the outer reaches of your mind.
Practising voodoo,
wearing spikes, suits,
bear claw ponchos, fur around their boots.
Letting out a *woo*! Chanting out a *ho*!
Carrying a nightstick, an urn
a cattle-prod and a two by four.
Acting the clown, shrinking heads,
getting Rowdy, resting in peace,
before rising from the dead.

It was a collar and elbow
before their suplexes, Perfect plexes,
sleepers and awakenings.
They went over the ropes, escaped cages.
Only a Brain could weasel their way out,
when a Monsoon's Irresistible force
met an immovable object.
It was such a Rush, it left them Bushwhacked
from clotheslines, back drops, D.D.Ts,
until the referee counted to three,
strapping winged eagle in victory feeling,
other laid flat, staring at the ceiling.

A New Generation arrived,
with a revolutionary force tilting to one side.
Going In Your House,
where Harts stepped out of shadows
to become kings on a throne,
where Harts executed immortality
to become champions on their own.

Yellow fever became a pink and black attack,
Warrior charged turned Diesel powered,
digging Macho now oozing Machismo.
From a Kid to an ironman in sixty-two,
a boyhood dream finally came true.

The tides began to Turn(er)
in a New World Order, a Blayze of destruction,
to crumble the Federation.
Until the call was made behind the curtain,
dialling 3:16 on a Ringmaster,
to a Stone Cold answer.
A Rocky start to knowing their role,
Sunny days were ahead with a Dust of Gold.
USA versus Canada, gripped by Chyna.
From the backlot to the boiler room,
the Man was screwed, the Kid was through,
all that remained was 'Attitude'.

Attitude scratched to a bloody scar,
to the bottom line
if you smell what I'm cookin.
With Nations, Corporations,
crotch chopping D-Generations.
Brothers of Destruction
playing The Game for all Mankind.
There was no tender loving care,
by those carrying tables, ladders, and chairs,
by those locked inside the cell.
Good god almighty you had to 'get it'.
If not, there was no chance in hell.

An Invasion led to a dose of poison,
an Icon vs Icon,
the Evolution, an Extension
towards a Ruthless Aggression,
bottled in a Lita of Stratusfaction.
The Kid returned home
to a language of Thuganomics,
with Money in the Bank,
seeing Animals, Killers, Big Evils.
Time to get Rated 'R', to get the 'F' out
for the next big thing.
Oh, its true, it was damn true.

What a manoeuvre! the Wrestle Mania.
The greatest show in sports entertainment.
I'll never fuhgeddaboudit,
then, now, forever.
It was Raw, a War, a Smackdown
in winter Rumbles, Summer Slams.
A Survivor Series
for those Kings of the Ring.
Anything can happen,
when the world is watching.
Anything can happen,
when you believe in wrestling.

Stage Four

Family: The Parts

Part 3296

You did all a grandad would,
no matter we didn't share blood.
Showing me love,
walking by my side
as we picked blackberries
behind the old rugby club.

Crushed under pits,
leaving half a stomach,
faded sound,
reliving time underground.
Aided by the box on your chest,
like plans for a bomb blast.

Making me forget the past,
wanting to be like you in the future.
Contented on leathered cracks,
'suppin tay', smoking away.
You were 'awreet', riding along paths,
with no intention of turning back.

This was a moment together, to treasure,
before illness took you away forever

But you are still here,
with your broad tone
echoed in my mind.
I have my memories –
you did all a grandad would,
no matter we didn't share blood.

Part 26996

You did all a mum would,
no matter we didn't share blood.
Showing me love,
sitting by my side,
as I ate chopped up eggs
from the broken brown cup.

You held my hand
on the first school day,
took air from my armbands.
There's no such word as can't
is what you always told me,
what you always taught me.

Protecting me from the past,
unable to see you in the future.
Forever remaining your special child.
Walking down those stairs
as your eyes filled, your arms opened,
embracing you in your final days.

This was a moment together, to treasure,
before illness took you away forever.

But you are still here,
with your smile in photographs,
with your words carrying me through.
I have my memories –
you did all a mum would,
no matter we didn't share blood.

A Sound Without Voice

I saw the spasm in your face,
heard the crunch in your throat,
before you left in the middle of the night.
Grieving in irritation,
chased by patterns,
by repetitions.
Unable to listen
to those lips, those fingertips.
I couldn't tell you my pain,
I had never heard of this.
We were suffering in silence
every single day,
spreading from our hearts,
rising above,
drifting away.

Stage Five

A Part

Sitting within four walls,
adjusting to the cracks.
Trapped in a place,
lost in a space,
that didn't even belong.

Detached in the attached,
childhood home held so close
in the hands of strangers.
Passing without a step on the path,
on a new route, from a different map.

I made a version of home
bringing past to a new stage –
sofas, sideboards, carpets, curtains.
My new life had become flat.
I knew what being apart meant.

No longer residing down the meade,
just a guest on a street,
with memories stored in boxes.
Drenching my pillow, wishing to drown,
to rivers where my childhood was found.

Sentence Order

THE DOOR LOCKED. BARRING ME FROM. A NORMAL LIFE. AWAY FROM KEYS. AWAY FROM LIGHTS. AWAY FROM THOUGHTS. AWAY FROM REPEATS. I COULDN'T STOP. LOSING THE CONTROL. LOSING MY GRIP. I COULDN'T STOP. I DIDN'T KNOW. WHAT IT WAS. I NEEDED CHANGE. TURN A CORNER. I WAS STANDING. AT AN ANGLE. ONE WAY ROAD. A JOURNEY LOST. BLIND TO SEE. WHAT WAS REAL. I COULDN'T FEEL. WHEN MY LIFE. WASN'T IN ORDER. HOW COULD I. BREAK THE CYCLE. WHEN THE WHEELS. KEPT ON TURNING. I SPOKE OUT. BUT NO ONE. HEARD MY VOICE. I COULD ONLY. STARE RIGHT DOWN. AT THE ABUSE. ON MY BLOODY. RED HANDS. STOP.

Stage Six

A Voice Without Sound

It was indistinct,
it was exposure
at the door,
recordings of smiles
lying on the floor.
I didn't know where to start.
Hallucination had turned
into deterioration,
making me lose the part,
the ability to speak.
Weighed down,
leaning towards
voiceless grief,
disabled speech,
with no words for the chords.

Family: The Parts

Part 8707

You did all a dad would,
no matter we didn't share blood.
Showing me love,
walking by my side,
as we carried soil
down the old railway line.

Working mornings, afternoons, nights.
Going to lengths,
riding with me for miles.
Putting a roof over my head,
sunburn on my skin,
presents under the tree.

Protecting me from the past,
seeing me into the future,
as we stood side by side
re-bonding on our turnstiles.
Basking in our club's celebrations,
weathering the storm of relegations.

This was a moment together, to treasure,
before illness took you away forever.

But you are still here,
with your chain resting as my wedding ring,
as you rest your eyes.
I have my memories –
you did all a dad would
no matter we didn't share blood.

Part 231208

You did all a grandma would,
no matter we didn't share blood.
Showing me love,
sitting by my side,
making up stories
about the girl who had to hide.

Living in the back room,
on patterned cushions.
History in your wrinkled hands
for all you had carried,
history in your wrinkled face
for all you had travelled.

Helping me understand the past,
grounding me for the future.
Carrying on without a daughter, son,
stories about those who had gone.
We connected by grief,
as you became a second mum.

This was a moment together, to treasure,
before illness took you away forever.

But you are still here
with stories I can tell,
as you did for me.
I have my memories –
you did all a grandma would
no matter we didn't share blood.

Part 24752365

You are all(ways) here,
with what you gave in the past.
Holding it in the present
carrying it in my future
as a family would,
with or without blood.

I Need Help

For years,
for months,
for weeks,
for minutes,
staring at a face
in total reflection.
Swimming in emotion
to drown myself.
Standing in flames
to burn myself.
Sitting in pain
to hurt myself,
to understand myself.
For one last time.
After all that time.
Before time.

The Journey Between

16:19 – 04:25

16:19   Leaning on railings at the station,
        at the end of my journey,
        the end of my days
        with lacklustre grades.
        It was never going to be the same
        as you waved over.

17:26   On a new journey
somewhere unknown.
I had a feeling lost inside,
I should have realised
it was the new forever in the haze.

19:09   Things slowly faded away
as I clamped my foot,
holding cash under rocks,
before the real world hit me
like a ton of bricks.
Pushing me forward,
unable to find my way back
to who I used to be.

16:19   I was in need of education.
I had all the weight of the words,
but they couldn't connect.
I needed more time
to read the chapters and stages,
but the wind had blown
flipping over pages,
in the departures and separations.

21:03   I wanted to travel,
arrive to where dreams were made,
but I fell asleep,
drifting away,
hoping someday
you would find me.

17:20 I couldn't find the communication,
to step off,
to turn back,
to go home.
This uncomfortable journey
took me to places
where I felt so alone

19:03 social security,

19:10 insurance claims,

19:20 delivering tellies,

20:21 packing fruit in classes,

21:22 reporting lab tests,

03:25 before the carrot dangled
in the telecoms veg patch.

00:00 Finding myself without a role,
signing myself on the dole.
Floating in procrastination,
drowning in masturbation,
with no shore in sight
rescuing me to a re-creation.

00:01 Out of work,
out of money,
out of ideas.
I couldn't piss in a pot,
but the watering can
held the change
for the bread, tea,
eviction noticed me,
but I went back to bed.

00:12   I gave that
which should've been saved.
She looked for a father,
I needed my mother.
I was weak, vulnerable,
unable to lift
from the pit
in my stomach.

01:12   A new family arrived.
I thought it was how to feel,
but I needed MY family,
I needed what was real.

02:09   I had to compute
to save me, help me
find the keys,
to control,
to alter,
to delete.

04:25   I had to break away,
to get away
to a different destination,
from a new connection.

IN THE MATTER OF (¹)

.... A CHILD.

The Journey Between

04:25 – 19:40

04:25   On a journey to start again,
            for somewhere to begin,
            to meet you on the other side
            in a different world.
            It was never going to be the same
            now it was over,
            fading into beautiful light.

04:04   Cheating for experience,
under influence,
to put 'love' in the past,
to live in the present,
to feel the independence.
Refreshed, smelling fresh
for the opposite sex.

00:02   My eyes opened.
I had no time,
I had to stop my life
withering away.

06:04   I was lost in the fun,
lost in the sun,
changing to become,
changing to be someone,
changing to be somewhere
to finally show my face again.
Walking with money in my pocket,
putty in my hair,
I thought I'd worked it all out
so, I didn't need to care.

16:05   Then I saw your glow
on a Spanish evening.
Taking your hand
as you took me
to a different meaning.
Questioning
will I ever see you again?
But you followed me back
with the sun in your eyes.

03:07   I returned to the station
on a different journey,
as the wave over
became the flow from the sea.
My heart outpoured
washing both our feet,
as you saw me
for who I was.

03:31   I knelt down
at your feet,
at the empire.

10:10   Then I began to write words
in my rehabilitation,

12:12   honouring my words
to show in devotion,

13:34   honouring those words
to showcase in creation.
Finally walking
to my destination,

19:40   the fortieth stage
of my graduation.

Stage Seven

Austin

Shaped in Texas,
gifted out of Grandma's will.
The other brother,
the other border
from the Hudson River.
Coming home, this grizzled red,
bringing me out of wreckage,
out of my bed,
to put one foot
in front of the other.

Early whimpers in the night,
wet patches on the floor,
bravery to the stairs
through the bathroom door.
Stepping out, breathing in,
breathing out, stepping in
dew, drizzle, sleet,
bounding under pads,
squelching under foot,
four paws and two feet.

Old Age is a Pain

Old age is a pain in the arse,
in the back,
in the teeth grinning
behind chipped glass.
In thinking it's Sunday,
it's Selfridges,
in the pills to help you sleep
to help you go
to help you stop.
In asking for a lift home,
for a lift upstairs,
for the bed to be downstairs.

Old age is a pain in the room
you are now living in,
falling in,
hoisted in.
In the room
full of faces,
waiting for a face
you don't remember,
you forget,
you forget to remember.
In waiting for the pain to end,
in the end.

Un-Frigid

Standing dressed in white
as a virgin bride,
but always turned on like a sex addict.
Coming to light when you open me,
looking up and down
to-ma-toes.

Other faces around
can only stare in jealousy –
fatty has no dish to clean,
pervert has no underwear to sniff,
shrivelling spinster
has nothing to touch.

You can forget those huge chests
as I am well stacked,
more than enough for you.
So, bring your packed meat,
open my drawers,
i'll keep it hard underneath.

For I am your dairy queen
milking you dry,
as you unload your cream on my top shelf,
your juice in my tight slots.
If you find the front spot,
I will gush my liquid for you.

But don't think you can butter me up,
I'm fully in charge, totally un-frigid,
making you rigid just looking at me,
staying cool as the cucumber inside me.
I'll always make you come,
to fill me up, to eat me out.

Wasted

I was thirty when I called time,
totally teetotal,
a non-alcoholic drinker,
taking others home
as the designated driver.
A choice,
a decision,
not for medicine,
not for religion,
not even for the taste.
For a shot, at culture,
ingrained in souls,
in hearts and minds,
filling society's hole.
Life has a lot to give,
drinking, socialising,
they're not mutually exclusive.
I didn't want to waste my time,
I didn't want to play the game,
I didn't want to forget my name.
Happy hour on my watch,
striking away at gin o'clock.
Bottled impurities,
glasses half full
of empty promises.

Words that regurge
plastered and trashed,
words in the unheard,
brought down to earth.
Drowning in nausea,
regretting the sound and sight
of the inside coming out,
turning into someone I'm not.
I'm a thinker, a dreamer,
an observer, a writer
keeping to straight lines,
hoping my words make sense.
I'd be wasted as a drinker.

Fall in Love

I waited at the window for you to fall,
away from heat so stifling,
longing for colours autumnal
clearing the air so suffocating.
A summer's day cannot compare
with the way you dance in your hazelnut dress,
for the way your soul doth bare,
to shake spear the sky I must confess
thou art more lovely in every way,
as your elegant tones began to unfold,
you drifted away,
leaving me in the cold.
At the window memories will retain,
at the window you will fall again.

Stage Eight

Blackpool

Blackest of pools,

darkest of waters,

bringing to shore,

drowning in tears.

Poverty behind the promenade,

every illuminating yard,

people deprived,

nowhere to stay,

nowhere to hide.

Laid down like trays on a beige buffet.

Vacant eyes, hunched body,

shadowed by no vacancy signs,

buried by rock stick sellers,

candy floss floggers.

Gypsy Lavinia is reading palms,

when all they need is a hand,

when all they need is change.

It isn't fun, it isn't fair

when reading between the lines,

when seeing what's in front of you,

sitting in the cracks of their home,

waiting to fill the gap in their heart.

Free

I remember how you used to rhyme,
walking with me to the end of the line.
The way your words could undress
the way your words could unstress.
I felt your beats, your rhythm
making my heart go dum-de-dum.
I thought we were on the same page,
I thought we were going the same way.
Written in the stars,
in a world that was ours,
holding you in my hand,
until you slipped through like grainy sand.

I read your words 'I am bic'
until you ran out,
leaving a mark on me,
dipping yourself in another form,
playing between the sheets.
I know I restricted your flow,
I know my schemes held you back.
I just needed commitment,
but you put the brakes on,
driving away in free verse.
I wish I could let it all go
but I'm lost for words.

In the Middle

In the middle of the churchyard,
silenced by the departed
years unearthed,
rising from ashes
from where it all started;
the eggs in the cup,
the sailor on the ship,
slipping hands to slipping sounds
down disinfected corridors.

Nakedness to the outside,
young hearts at the left side
in the altogether.
A stillness in time,
a bonding, a belonging,
travelling forever
before the last ride.
I remember those growing stages,
walking in these middle ages.

But I'm still the child in an adult,
the boy in a man,
with blood
waiting for the heart to beat,
with voice
waiting to finally speak.
In the middle of the churchyard
I am the only one alive,
but buried underneath.

Stage Nine

An Education

How many downs can you lock?
How many frowns can unlock
the emotion behind the mask
on a child's face?
Behind the screens
as the only means
of communication,
these were the few,
as the rest of the classes
stayed at home with the masses.

Entrances behind exits,
barriers in front of bubbles,
for air to breathe,
distance to leave.
These were the key
workers for Maths, English, Art.
'Sir, when will Covid end?'
'I wish I knew where to start'.
All they could feel was separation,
learning their way in a new education.

Halcyon (elm)

Moving on is
Easy to say when you are not
Lost in what has been found.
Aching heart
Now back in time,
Crying within strangers' walls.
Hopes and fears
Opened a river of tears,
Longing to be living in those
Years gone by.

Stage Ten

The Haven

Midnight's walk in the dreary, pondering the soul of weak
and weary
living within empty bottles of LENOR.[1]
While he nodded, nearly dropping, suddenly there came a
knocking,
as if someone was gently helping, helping at his front door.
'Tis some fucking nuisance,' he muttered, knocking on
my door,
'the Jesus force or another charity whore.'

On his own on a cold December
with each faded freebie, lying upon his floor.
Never would come tomorrow – his vow to return his borrow,
heart-breaking books resembled his sorrow – sorrow for the
world unexplored.
For his lack of care and pungent odour whom some 'Galore' –
could be here for evermore.

And the sadness rustling behind the curtains
saddened me – filled me with the errors in society
who ignore
the beating of his heart. I stood repeating, until he answered
'Who's that bastard at my door?
Another do-gooding arsehole thinking they know more.
Piss off, don't come back anymore.'

---

[1] Lenor® – Proctor & Gamble product

My soul felt stronger, I hesitated no longer,
'Sir, let me help you, I implore';
but maybe he was napping or on the Poe
and couldn't get past the clutter at the toilet door.
Suddenly I realised the unlocked, opening his front door;
just hoarding there and nothing more.

Deep into this disorder, I could stand it no longer,
questioning,
understanding no other had understood before;
everything was discarded or broken, around the tins and
tokens.
I didn't know his name, so I whispered 'Galore'
and an echo murmured back — 'Galore?!
my name is Edgar, that's fucking sure!'

In his kitchen turning, I could smell the burning,
I could hear the smoke alarm beeping;
surely that is from the oven, a strudel or lattice?
Let the cushion flap away,
let the smoke out of the window,
let in the wind and nothing more.

I rolled up the blinds, when with some much dust
making me splutter.
Opening the light to the haven he'd been living in.
Never before the loss of his lady perched aside the living
room door —
perched above pizza menus, leaflets from the store —
it used to perch, sit, now nothing more.

This decayed bird in the corroded cage, realising
need for her grave to lie with dignity.
Thou sure were a brave one,
now ghostly in the haven, fluttering above the floor –
her name, 'Chipper', was irony for sure,
note the haven 'never no more'.

Much I held my breath to the ungodly foul smell,
the answers have meaning – this man is like Eeyore,
but we cannot stress that no body of being,
should be given up for evermore.
Even the vain standing at the mirror,
this is mental health at its core.

But this haven, unable to rise like a flaccid one to a bust.
If his soul could speak, help him outpour,
nothing would go any further I uttered –
'I know this place is cluttered,
but all my friends have fucking left –
my hopes went with them, never coming back anymore.'

Broken by the tear in his eye, offering a tissue,
'what you need is to take stock
of what you could have in store.
You are the master to stop this potential disaster,
Heaven Knows You Are Miserable Now,
you could be This Charming Man for evermore.'

But his haven was leading him to withering.
I wheeled his chair with seated cushion,
now sinking just like his heart.
The suffering and tears were in the outpour
of this gangly and ghostly man nicknamed 'Galore'.
'Edgar,' I croaked, 'please don't ignore'.

I sat among the engagement rings, no words expressing
of these diamond eyes that glisten, who for I am unsure.
The cushioned velvet and ripped lining was that of a bear –
named 'Glow-Ted'.
The button still intact, which I went to press,
Edgar spoke; 'Bastard thing doesn't work anymore.'

I thought to cleanse the air, perfume it from incense;
'Sandalwood by Selfridges' would help but not of the tinkles
on the rough floor.
'Edgar!' I shouted, 'God has lent thee angels, angels to send
thee for respite,
either that or social services to wash your clothes in
LENOR.'[2]
'Oh fuck off, angels my arse, they'd never get the stains out,
that's for sure!
Note my smell "old cheese with manure."'

---

[2] Lenor® – Proctor & Gamble product

'I ain't lost it yet,' said Edgar. 'Social services are a thing of
evil, a thing of the devil! –
some tosser here, some arsehole there,
reminding me of my desolate land.
This home isn't a horror – of that I am sure.
So, what if I have too many disposable razors?
Note the unshaven "never sore".'

'I am not for profit,' he said, 'for ones to revel in my misery –
telling me my soul is distant and full of sorrow.
I wouldn't mind a maiden who was willing to be a whore,
clasp around my raging body,
not affected by my sores,
asking her, "Ever done it up the back door?"'

'So this is where we must part, young fiend!' Edgar shrieked –
'get thee back to your wife, your children, your life so pure!
Don't take anything so much as a token that lies,
I have friggin spoken! Leave my loneliness broken –
quit the bollocks and get out my door!
I have no need for anyone anymore.'

And the haven, along with him, never flitting, just sitting,
pallid face, feet of callus, willing to endure.
Eyes seeping from a demon. He's not dreaming.
Bring light over him, stream him down the river of hope,
bring his shadow from the floor, away from the soul of Galore,
Edgar can be lifted for evermore.

Meh!

Are you listening?
To silence,
to apathy,
where indifference stands
in the middle,
sits on the fence
shrugging its shoulders.
Meh isn't listening.
It doesn't care about you,
about me,
meh doesn't care about meh,
meh can't be bothered,
isn't invested,
isn't interested.
Meh doesn't even like this poem
or even the words.
You may not either,
maybe you do?
Who cares… it's all meh,
and you are a-hem.

Live

Wandering lonely in the cloud,
like distant daffodils in the field of screens.
Drifting away online,
unseen from the breeze.
Stretched updates in a timeline
with never ending tweets.
Pictures worth a thousand words
lost in self reflections.

What sap of energy
in the forest of imitation?
Roots to the un-growth,
soiled by instant stories.
Connected to Wi-Fi,
disconnected from you and I.
There are settings,
but we have our place.

Life is rolling down the river
as the need for feed
streams in habitual scrolling.
Hands can hold a world of connection
but separation is slipping
in front of our eyes.
Words are worth more in the daffodils,
ready to be alive, not waiting to go live.

Stage Eleven

This is Literally a Poem

This is a poem, literally.
It is literally literary
about the word literally.
Other words have died,
I read them in the obituaries.

Goodbye to actually,
so long to completely,
indisputably, definitively.
TTFN to really,
R.I.P to the letter.

There was literally a million words.
I literally couldn't believe it.
They literally blew my mind,
literally made my head explode
and I literally died.

Unequivocally to unquestionably,
words I'd never seen, literally.
I saw figuratively, metaphorically,
but I love the word literally,
I just do it habitually.

I know the word has been abused,
I know it has been overused,
but its literally the only word I choose.
This poem wouldn't have been written, literally
without the word, literally!

Those Fucking People

There are those people every day
always getting in the fucking way,
rushing to consume from life's buffet.
Completely draining, taking their toll,
with tiring sound, letting everyone down
like a deflated sex doll.
Forever telling you what they think,
walking around like their shit doesn't stink.

Loving the sound of their own voice,
living where money talks, bullshit walks,
with no highway down their way.
Swimming freely in the hypocri-sea,
wrapping agendas in principles,
hiding their body of loopholes,
all joined together,
shitting through the same arseholes.

Sleeping in the antiquated,
waking up in the opinionated.
Hammering through, nailing their views,
not one of them on the level.
Just a bunch of fucking tools
thinking they have the answers,
never reading questions in the book,
with their cock in, but no balls to fuck.

Too many faces, too many voices,
too many names, too many noises.
How can I live in the authenti-city
when there are too many cunt-ries
in my space, in my fucking face?
I wish those people farewell,
they are a pain in the arse
and as for me… fucking hell!

Arnie

Shaping chapters
with Sterling's priceless story.
It was now or never
for the other border,
for Austin's brother.
Coming home, this grizzled tan
Scottish, Smallish, Loish.
A Christmas present,
wrapped in blankets,
wrapped in future plans.

Futures vision 20:20
was broken down, locked down.
Five months old, fractured in growth,
crated to recover.
Developing with distancing,
developing an understanding
that the cracks in the beginning
made him completely whole.
Bounding over life's hurdles,
the biggest heart in this happy little soul.

Stage Twelve

Leigh

Never go back,
but how could I not
move forward?
Re-visit my roots,
re-visit those routes,
walking in new boots.
It opened up
Mum's dying embrace,
echoing through close-knit arms
standing at the bus stop.

Back to the school,
reliving the marks
left on me.
Fresh paint on those walls,
new subjects in those rooms.
Walking down corridors,
lower, upper, feeling in-between.
Standing in the hall,
standing at the same spot
where I left at sixteen.

Back to the town,
remembering the ways
I was uniformed in Boardmans,
United in Footwear.

Spinning between the gates,
standing in that Union spot
for Yates Greer pies, Waterfield's cakes,
Birchall's magazines, Chamley's books.
Wishing Sweet Regards
to Mum's special shop.

Back to the home,
reminiscing about those days
at the surface of the river,
rising above the brook.
Red Waters, Greenways,
between the smokey ginnel,
redcurrant scent Avenue.
Looking out of my window
to the roots of Elmridge,
in sunset dusk from Lilford woods.

Back to the memories,
rewinding the years,
playing back those tears.
You can't live in the past,
but where is the future
when the present stops serving?
Unwrapping to an empty gift.
I go back to go forward,
standing under whispering blossom
of those who loved back.

...Before

Inborn, body ready to happen,
back to where I began.
The inconceivable meaning.
To lose myself in nature's recorded,
forty years since I was adopted.

Digging up what's buried within,
my scattered foundation,
broken, neglected in rubbled haze,
the false start, the finished truth,
sitting in a folder for decades.

To uncover beyond my birth name,
uncover beyond fraud and pain
written down. The life I cannot explain.
To find the grounding,
to build an understanding.

Of the life unplanned,
in the life now as a man.
Words unleashed after all this time,
letters in the before, in the aftermath,
to meet who I was back then.

F.I.L.E

FOUND OUT THE MYSTERY
FOUND OUT MY HISTORY
FOUND OUT WHO I WAS
FOUND OUT WHAT I HAD LOST

IDENTITY AT 3.25
IDENTITY AT 7LBS
IDENTITY AT 12/02
IDENTITY IN 3 WKS.

LEAVING WHAT WAS PARALYSED
LEAVING WHAT WAS INSUFFICIENT
LEAVING WHAT WAS RETARDED
LEAVING WHAT I EVER MEANT

ECHOES IN WHAT I HAD FOUND
ECHOES IN LETTERS
ECHOES OF THEIR VOICE
ECHOES OF THEIR SOUND

An unspeakable,
freed from inside the chamber —
the identity...

References

Keane, *Somewhere Only We Know*, Hopes And Fears, Island, 2004

Keane, *Bend And Break*, Hopes And Fears, Island, 2004

Keane, *We Might As Well Be Strangers*, Hopes And Fears, Island, 2004

Keane, *Everybody's Changing*, Hopes And Fears, Island, 2004

Keane, *Your Eyes Open*, Hopes And Fears, Island, 2004

Keane, *She Has No Time*, Hopes And Fears, Island, 2004

Keane, *Can't Stop Now*, Hopes And Fears, Island, 2004

Keane, *Sunshine*, Hopes And Fears, Island, 2004

Keane, *This Is The Last Time*, Hopes And Fears, Island, 2004

Keane, *Untitled 1*, Hopes And Fears, Island, 2004

Keane, *Bedshaped*, Hopes And Fears, Island, 2004

Oasis, *Hello*, (What's The Story) Morning Glory?, Creation, 1995

Oasis, *Roll With It*, (What's The Story) Morning Glory?, Creation, 1995

Oasis, *Wonderwall*, (What's The Story) Morning Glory?, Creation, 1995

Oasis, *Don't Look Back In Anger*, (What's The Story) Morning Glory?, Creation, 1995

Oasis, *Hey Now,* (What's The Story) Morning Glory?, Creation, 1995

Oasis, *Some Might Say*, (What's The Story) Morning Glory?, Creation, 1995

Oasis, *Cast No Shadow*, (What's The Story) Morning Glory?, Creation, 1995

Oasis, *She's Electric*, (What's The Story) Morning Glory?, Creation, 1995

Oasis, *Morning Glory*, (What's The Story) Morning Glory?, Creation, 1995

Oasis, *Champagne Supernova*, (What's The Story) Morning Glory?, Creation, 1995

The Smiths, *Heaven Knows I'm Miserable Now*, Hatful of Hollow, Rough Trade, 1984

The Smiths, *This Charming Man*, Rough Trade, 1983

Benny Hill, *Ernie (The Fastest Milkman In The West)*, Words and Music, 1971

Carry On films, Norman Hudis (1958-1962), Talbot Rothwell (1963-1974), Anglo-Amalgamated, The Rank Organisation, 1958-1978

Edgar Allen Poe, *The Raven*, 1845

Clement Clarke Moore, *A Visit From St, Nicholas/ 'Twas The Night Before Christmas*, 1823

William Wordsworth, *I Wandered Lonely as a Cloud (The Daffodills)*, 1807

William Shakespeare, *Sonnet 18*, 1609

Milton Keynes UK
Ingram Content Group UK Ltd.
UKHW021849250124
436727UK00014B/81/J